Saving Our World

HABITAT
PROTECTION

Natalie Smith

Marshall Cavendish
Benchmark
New York

Marshall Cavendish Benchmark
99 White Plains Road
Tarrytown, NY 10591
www.marshallcavendish.us

All Internet addresses were available and accurate when this book was sent to press.

Library of Congress Cataloging-in-Publication Data

Smith, Natalie, 1983-

　Habitat protection / by Natalie Smith.

　p. cm. -- (Saving our world)

　Includes bibliographical references and index.

　ISBN 978-0-7614-3225-8

1.　Habitat conservation--Juvenile literature.　I. Title.

　QH75.S577 2009

　333.95--dc22

　2008014555

The photographs in this book are used by permission and through the courtesy of:

Half Title: Pichugin Dmitry/ Shutterstock
Pichugin Dmitry/Shutterstock: 4-5, Tyrone Turner/Getty Images: 6-7, Q2A Media Image Bank: 6, Maugli/Shutterstock: 8-9, Galina Barskaya/Shutterstock: 10-11, Eric Gevaert/ Shutterstock: 12-13, Igor Kozel/ Shutterstock: 14-15, Emilia Kun/Shutterstock: 16-17, Mike Flippo/Shutterstock: 18, J.L.Bulcão/Istockphoto: 18-19, Juniors Bildarchiv/ Photolibrary: 20-21, Sanruft/Istockphoto: 22-23, Pichugin Dmitry/Shutterstock: 24-25, Pichugin Dmitry/Shutterstock: 26-27, Mike Greenslade / Alamy: 28-29.

Cover photo: Burgess Michele/ Photolibrary; Arnold John Labrentz/ Shutterstock; Oleg Prikhodko/Istockphoto.

Illustrations: Q2AMedia Art Bank

Created by: Q2A Media

Creative Director: Simmi Sikka

Series Editor: Maura Christopher

Series Art Director: Sudakshina Basu

Series Designers: Dibakar Acharjee, Joita Das, Mansi Mittal, Rati Mathur and Shruti Bahl

Series Illustrator: Abhideep Jha and Ajay Sharma

Photo research by Anju Pathak

Series Project Managers: Ravneet Kaur and Shekhar Kapur

Printed in Malaysia

1 3 5 6 4 2

CONTENTS

Our Habitats

Habitats are all around us. They are the natural environments where plants and animals make their home. Our planet is home to many kinds of habitats, from the deep ocean waters to the tall mountaintops.

The Right Conditions

Habitats provide the basic resources that living things need to survive. Food, air, and water are some examples of these supplies. But different living things have different needs. A habitat that is best for one species could be harmful to another. Polar bears, for instance, live in the Arctic, an ice-covered area around the North Pole. Their bodies are designed to keep warm in very cold temperatures. Many animals from other habitats could not survive in these extreme arctic conditions.

Humans have the greatest impact on habitats. If we don't change our actions, our planet may some day be unable to support life.

Endangered Habitats

Throughout the world, habitats face many threats. Some of these threats are from natural forces, such as earthquakes and fires. However, the most harmful threats are caused by human activity, such as clearing forests and polluting beaches with waste. People clearing forests and polluting beaches with waste are examples of this threat. When a habitat is destroyed, the plants and animals that once lived there are left homeless.

EYE-OPENER

Our planet is full of different **species**. This wide variety of life is known as **biodiversity**. Over the past one hundred years, wildlife has had a tough time keeping up with our changing world. When natural habitats are destroyed, populations of certain plant and animal species decline. Today, thousands of species are endangered. This means they are in danger of becoming extinct, or no longer existing anywhere in the world.

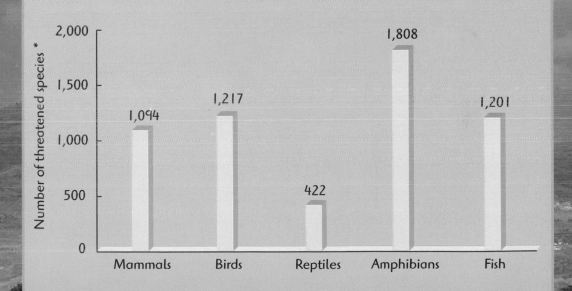

*This chart shows the number of vertebrate species that are listed as critically endangered, endangered, or vulnerable.

Source: 2007 International Union for the Conservation of Nature Red List.

Forming a Community

All plants and animals in a habitat depend on one another. Each species has a special place in the **food chain**. Some parts of certain plants, such as the leaves and roots, are edible. Some animals feed on these parts, while other animals eat the plant-eaters. If just one species of plant is wiped out, it can be damaging to several living things in a habitat.

Giraffes, elephants, and zebras share a habitat on the grasslands.

Climate Change

Global warming—the gradual increase in the Earth's temperature—is another factor that is changing our planet's habitats. Though natural causes can affect Earth's temperature, most scientists think that humans are causing **global warming**. People burn fossil fuels (oil, gas, and natural gas) to run their vehicles and for many other activities. This releases **greenhouse gases**, such as carbon dioxide, into the air. These gases trap heat in the atmosphere, which causes the atmosphere to grow warmer. If this climate change continues, it could put most of the species on the Earth at risk.

A bird walks through trash in a creek. Many of the world's beaches are littered with waste.

QUESTION TIME ?

How does the increasing human population affect our planet?

Every day, the number of people living on Earth continues to grow. As a result, humans require more land for places to live and work. Many habitats are destroyed to meet the growing demands of people.

Fresh Water

Bodies of water containing very low levels of salt and other minerals make up the world's freshwater habitats. Most lakes, rivers, ponds, and wetlands are fresh water habitats.

Lakes and Ponds

Lakes and ponds are bodies of freshwater that fill **depressions** in the Earth's surface. In the United States, these freshwater sources supply 70 percent of the water used in our country for drinking, watering crops, and producing power. They also provide a habitat for many animals and plants, including fish, turtles, and water lilies.

Rivers and Streams

Rivers and streams are bodies of flowing water. These habitats do not collect water as lakes and ponds do. They carry fresh water from a body of land, such as a mountain range, to a lake or ocean. Rivers and streams are important to the planet for many reasons. For example, they help fish **migrate** between water systems.

Turquoise Lake in Colorado is one of the freshwater habitats found in the United States.

Wetlands

Wetlands, such as swamps and marshes, are areas that are soaked with water at least part of the year. Some wetlands are formed inland and contain fresh water. Others form in coastal areas where fresh water merges with the ocean's salt water. Wetlands are home to a variety of plants and animals, including cordgrass, frogs, snakes, alligators, and many fish.

EYE-OPENER

Over the past four hundred years, more than half of the original wetlands in the United States have been drained or turned into fields. The loss of wetlands has a serious effect on the thousands of species that call wetlands their home. More than one-third of all threatened and endangered species in the United States live only in wetlands.

Pollution

Pollution is a big threat to freshwater habitats. Dumping wastes into water is a cheap and easy way to dispose of it. But polluted water can poison plants and animals when it enters their environment. It is also harmful to humans. In **developed countries**, water is usually **purified** before it is used for drinking. But for some poor countries, this process is too costly. More than one billion people worldwide do not have access to safe water.

Freshwater Supply

Every living thing on Earth needs water to live. But only about 3 percent of the world's water is fresh water. Much of that is frozen in **ice caps** and glaciers. Less than 1 percent is left for the people, plants, and animals. Although water is a **renewable resource**, human consumption is beginning to reduce this limited supply.

Many of the animals that live in freshwater habitats are killed by pollutants such as oil, sewage, and chemicals.

How much water does an average person need a day?

People require less than one gallon of water a day to stay alive. But in the United States, the average person uses more than 100 gallons of water each day. In countries where water is not readily available, people use far less. In Africa, many people have to walk long distances to collect water. The average African family uses only about five gallons of water each day.

As human populations continue to rise, so do the pressures on the world's limited freshwater supply. This map shows the areas of the world where the levels of fresh water are already low and the areas where it is starting to run low.

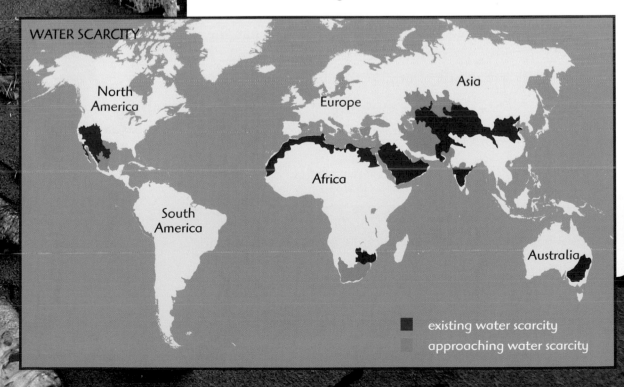

WATER SCARCITY

North America

Europe

Asia

Africa

South America

Australia

■ existing water scarcity

□ approaching water scarcity

Marine Habitats

Oceans cover more than two-thirds of the planet. They form the largest habitat on Earth. Other smaller marine habitats, such as coral reefs and coastal zones, exist within oceans.

Saltwater Habitats

The marine habitat is mostly made up of the Pacific, Atlantic, Indian, Arctic, and Southern oceans. Most seas are part of this habitat, too. They are usually part of a larger ocean. For example, the Caribbean Sea is part of the Atlantic Ocean.

Marine Life

The ocean supports a wide range of creatures. Its major food producers are known as algae. These small rootless plants, such as seaweed, grow in water or on damp surfaces. Small floating animals known as zooplankton eat the algae. Jellyfish are an example of zooplankton. Fish in the ocean eat the zooplankton, and big fish eat smaller fish. Some large animals, such as the whale shark, also eat zooplankton.

Fishing can have a serious impact on the ocean's wildlife. Animals not meant for the net are often entangled by accident.

Overfishing

The largest threat to ocean life and habitats is overfishing. Millions of people around the world rely on fish for food. But fishing practices are not well monitored. As a result, humans are taking more fish out of the ocean than marine habitats can produce. The large reduction in fish populations is not only a concern for humans. It affects the entire ocean food chain. Marine species, such as seals and dolphins, are left with fewer fish to eat.

Coral Reefs

Coral reefs are underwater colonies made up of billions of colorful tiny animals called corals. They grow in warm, shallow waters. Coral reefs provide food and shelter for millions of marine species, including sea stars and clownfish. This habitat is very fragile. Pollution and other human activities have threatened or destroyed more than half the world's reefs.

QUESTION TIME ?

Why are coral reefs important?

Coral reefs are valuable for providing protection to ocean coastlines. They help break the power of waves during heavy storms. This protects the beaches from flooding and from erosion. Corals have also made important contributions to medicine. They are used in treatments for some diseases and health conditions.

Coasts

The coastal zone is the area where the ocean's water meets the sand. Though coasts make up 10 percent of the entire ocean environment, they are home to more than 90 percent of all marine species. Coral reefs are found in this zone. Because sunlight can reach parts of the shallow waters, plants can grow in this habitat. Of all the marine environments, the coastal zone has the most nutrients.

This coast in southwest England is one of the world's many marine habitats.

Ocean Pollution

Most of the waste that humans produce on land eventually ends up in the ocean. In addition, ships that travel through the waters can have accidental oil spills. Sometimes they dump waste overboard. Almost every marine animal is affected by these pollutants.

Forest Habitats

About one-third of the Earth's land is covered with forests. There are many kinds of forest habitats. The three major types are tropical rain forests, temperate forests, and coniferous forests.

Tropical Rain Forests

Tropical rain forests are located close to the **equator**. They have continually warm temperatures and receive heavy rainfall. The tops of the tallest trees in a rain forest form the **emergent layer**. The next layer is the **canopy**, which receives lots of sun. The lower trees make up the **understory** layer. The final layer is the forest floor, which is covered with roots. This layer gets little sun.

EYE-OPENER

Tropical rain forests once covered more than 6 million square miles of the Earth. Today, fewer than 3 million square miles remain. People cut down trees to clear land for farms and for lumber. The shrinking forests are of concern for wildlife and threaten their existence.

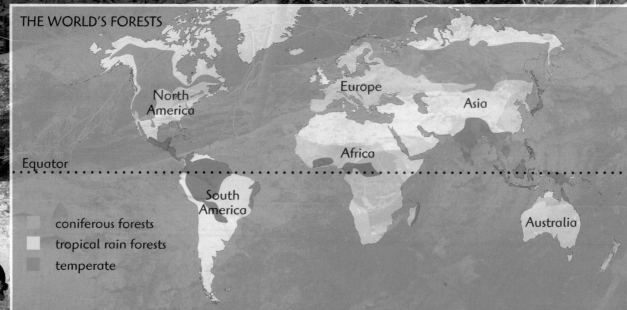

THE WORLD'S FORESTS

North America

Europe

Asia

Africa

Equator

South America

Australia

coniferous forests

tropical rain forests

temperate

Forest Life

Rain forests are home to many species of wildlife. Most animals live in the branches of the canopy where they can find food. Birds and small frogs live here, feeding on leaf-eating insects. Lizards and snakes feed on these animals. Jaguars and other big cats live on the branches of the understory. They drop to the ground when they spot their prey. Insects, small deer, rodents, and elephants are some of the animals occupying the forest floor.

Temperate Forests

Temperate forests grow in areas that have warm, wet summers and cold, snowy winters. Trees in temperate forests are deciduous, which means they lose their leaves in the fall. These trees include maple, oak, and walnut. Animal life in this habitat is not as diverse as in tropical rain forests. Deer, rabbits, foxes, and owls are some types of the wildlife that make their home in temperate forests.

Endangered Pandas

Giant pandas live in temperate forests in central China. The animals live almost exclusively on **bamboo**. But bamboo forests are disappearing. Today, only about 1,600 giant pandas are left in the wild. Many zookeepers and researchers are working to create new nature reserves to protect panda habitats.

QUESTION TIME ?

How can you help protect the world's forests?

One important and simple way you can help protect the remaining natural forests is by reducing your paper consumption. Only print paper from the computer that you really need. When you do print, set your printer to use both sides of the paper. Recycle the paper you can't reuse and donate wood products, such as furniture, that you no longer want.

Coniferous Forests

Coniferous forests grow in areas that have short summers and long, cold winters. Trees that grow here have needlelike leaves and cones instead of flowers. Pines, firs, and spruces are some of the trees that grow in coniferous forests. Moose, elk, squirrels, and blueberry plants can all be found there.

Sometimes forest fires are essential for forest rebirth, but fires can become a problem if they burn in the wrong places.

Grasslands

Grasslands are areas covered mostly by grass with few or no trees. They have many different names, including prairies, pampas, and savannas. Every continent except for Antarctica has grasslands.

Weather Conditions

Grasslands grow in areas that are too dry to produce a forest, but not dry enough to be deserts. In temperate grasslands, the summers are hot, the winters are cold, and there is little rainfall. Tropical grasslands are found in warm or hot climates that receive plenty of rain in the summer.

Grassland Destruction

Not much of the world's natural grassland remains. Grasslands are often converted into corn or wheat fields. This has pushed many animals out of their homes. In the United States, an estimated 20 to 30 million bison once existed in natural grasslands. Today, their numbers have been reduced to a few hundred thousand.

Wildlife

Grasslands include types of plants that are able to keep growing no matter how much animals feed on them. Animals such as zebras, antelopes, and buffalos feed on the grass. Predators include cheetahs, lions, and hyenas. They feed on plant-eaters in the habitat.

Not much of the world's natural grasslands remain. Their fertile soil is often converted into corn or wheat fields.

Tundra

Treeless plains found in the Arctic and on top of mountains are called tundra. The lands are covered in snow most of the year and the areas receive little rain. They are the coldest of all the habitats.

Arctic Tundra

The Arctic tundra is located in the northernmost regions of North America, Europe, and Asia surrounding the Arctic Ocean. Temperatures rarely reach above 45 degrees Fahrenheit (7.2 degrees Celsius). It is too cold for trees to grow here. Plants that grow—shrubs, mosses, and grass—have adapted by remaining small. Wolves, polar bears, caribou, and arctic moles and shrews are some of the animals that live in the tundra.

If too much of the frozen soil in the Arctic tundra melts, it could change forever what species are able to live there.

The tundra is one of the most sensitive habitats in the world. Warmer climates caused by global warming are threatening the tundra. The fall freeze is coming later in the year, and more ice is melting each summer. Scientists worry that these trends could change these regions and their species forever.

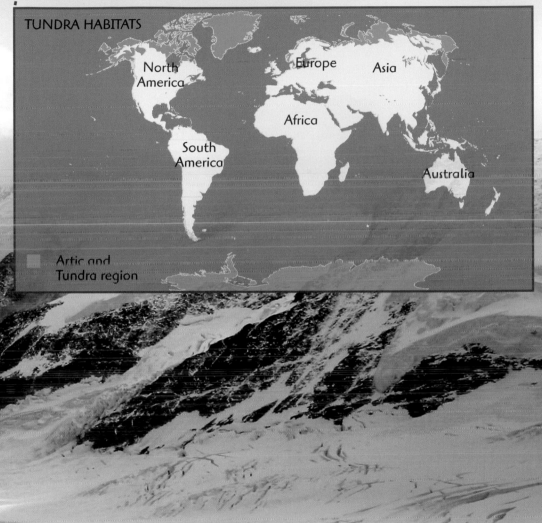

TUNDRA HABITATS

North America

Europe

Asia

Africa

South America

Australia

☐ Artic and Tundra region

Alpine Tundra

Alpine tundra is located on top of high mountains throughout the world. The climate and plant life in these regions is similar to the Arctic tundra. Mountain goats, sheep, and birds live in the alpine tundra.

Deserts

Deserts are the driest areas of the world. They cover about one-fifth of the Earth's surface. They can be hot or cold, but both types have little rainfall. Some deserts go several years without receiving any rain.

The camel is one of many animals that live in the desert. Desert animals have many adaptations that allow them to survive in harsh, dry conditions.

Varying Surfaces

Not all deserts are made up of sand. Some have flat, stony plains. Others consist of uneven, rocky hills and mountains. Antarctica, which is made up of snow and ice, is considered a desert. Most deserts are a combination of different landscapes.

EYE-OPENER

Higher temperatures caused by global warming threaten desert landscapes. The warm temperatures increase the number of **droughts**, which dry up water holes. These changes can have a serious effect on desert plant and animal life. Climate change and human activity are also causing more land to turn into deserts. This process is known as desertification, and it is occurring at an alarming rate.

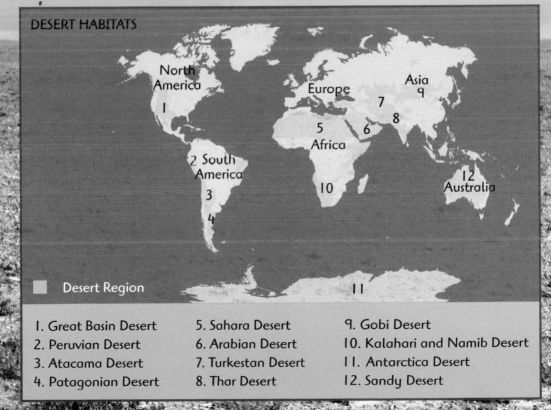

DESERT HABITATS

North America
1

2 South America
3
4

Europe
5
Africa

7
8
6

Asia
9

10

12
Australia

Desert Region

11

1. Great Basin Desert	5. Sahara Desert	9. Gobi Desert
2. Peruvian Desert	6. Arabian Desert	10. Kalahari and Namib Desert
3. Atacama Desert	7. Turkestan Desert	11. Antarctica Desert
4. Patagonian Desert	8. Thar Desert	12. Sandy Desert

Habitat Protection

If our planet is to continue to serve as a home for millions of species, then its habitats must be protected. The good news is that everyone has the power to affect these environments in positive ways. Even small changes can make a big difference.

Preserving Land

There are many groups worldwide that work to preserve habitats. One is the Wildlife Land Trust. They have contributed to the protection of habitats in thirty-three states and four foreign countries. On the group's land, no hunting is allowed and logging is limited. The Trust is one of the groups that worked for the permanent protection of nearly 10,000 acres of rain forest and related habitats in Belize, a country in Central America. They have made these areas safe from development or other destructive activities.

Elephants are one of the world's threatened species. There are laws in place worldwide to help protect the species.

Laws That Protect Habitats

Certain laws also help protect endangered land and wildlife. In October 1972, the U.S. government passed a law making it illegal to dump certain harmful materials in the ocean, such as industrial wastes. Before that time, few people thought about the harm that dumping such wastes in the ocean would cause. Similar rules also exist to protect endangered wildlife. One **treaty** bans 160 countries from trading more than 30,000 species of animals and plants.

EYE-OPENER

In the United States, the Endangered Species Act protects plants and animals that are at risk of becoming extinct. Bald eagles gained protection under the act in 1973. Before the act, fewer than five hundred breeding pairs were left in the United States because of habitat loss and other threats. Thanks to protection from the law, by 2006 their numbers had soared to almost 10,000 nesting pairs.

A Job for Everyone

Everyone can have a role in protecting habitats. Here are a few simple ways you can help:

- Recycle when possible and buy products made from recycled materials.

- Donate items that you no longer want to charity or to a thrift store.

- Promote biodiversity by planting trees and flowers.

- Respect wildlife. If you see a bird's nest, don't touch or disturb it. Don't pull flowers from the ground.

- Reduce water usage. Turn off the water when brushing your teeth, and don't take long showers.

- Walk or ride a bike for short trips.

- Don't litter. Help pick up trash by participating in a community trash clean-up day.

- Save energy. Turn off or unplug appliances and electronics when you leave a room. Using compact fluorescent light bulbs can also help save energy.

QUESTION TIME ?

What is a compact fluorescent light bulb?

A compact fluorescent light bulb is a type of light bulb that uses less energy than a traditional light bulb. Creating electricity adds greenhouse gases to the atmosphere. If every U.S. home switched five regular bulbs for five compact fluorescent bulbs, it would prevent more than one trillion pounds of greenhouse gases from entering the air each year.

Members of the group Surfers Against Sewage help clean up trash on a beach.

Adopting Habitats

Some groups help people protect areas of a natural habitat. The Nature Conservancy, for instance, has an Adopt-An-Acre Program. It allows people to donate money to "adopt" an acre of threatened rain forest. The donations help the group to protect and restore the region. The World Wildlife Fund and the National Wildlife Federation offer similar programs.

Act Now

Think about how to protect endangered habitats. Use that knowledge and share it with others. Every single person has the power to make changes, big and small, which can help save our environment. By working together, we can change our world!

Glossary

bamboo: A tropical plant with a hard, hollow stem.

biodiversity: The number and variety of species found within a specific area.

canopy: The layer in a forest below the emergent layer, which is formed by the leaves and branches of the tallest branches.

depression: A hollow or sunken area.

developed country: A country with high average incomes and well-developed services such as hospitals and schools.

drought: A long period of very dry weather.

emergent layer: The tallest layer in the rain forest. It is made up of the few very tall trees that grow higher than the canopy.

equator: An imaginary line between the middle of the Earth, halfway between the North and South Poles.

fertile: Rich in material needed to maintain plant growth.

food chain: A series of plants and animals in a community in which each one feeds on the one below it in the chain.

global warming: A gradual rise in the temperature of the Earth's atmosphere caused by gases such as carbon dioxide that collect in the atmosphere and prevent the Sun's heat from escaping.

greenhouse gases: Gases such as carbon dioxide and methane that are found in the Earth's atmosphere and help hold heat in.

ice cap: A dome-shaped ice mass that permanently covers a large area of land, such as a mountaintop.

migrate: To move from one country or region to another.

purify: To make something clean and free of any pollutants.

renewable resource: Any natural resource that can never be used up, such as wind and the Sun.

species: A single type of plant or animal that has common characteristics and is classified by a common name.

treaty: a formal written agreement between countries or governments.

understory: The layer in a forest formed by the leaves and branches of the smaller trees under the canopy.

Where to Find Out More

- Learn about the plants and animals that live in your neighborhood by typing in your zip code at www.enature.com.

- The National Wildlife Federations has up-to-date nature news and information on ways you can protect the environment at: www.nwf.org.

- The U.S. Environmental Protection Agency Web site for children offers information on how kids can make the environment cleaner at: www.epa.gov/kids.

- The U.S. Fish and Wildlife service offers information on habitats and the animals that live in them as well as news and information on the world's endangered species at: www.fws.gov.

- The World Wildlife Fund works to protect animals and their habitats around the world at: www.worldwildlife.org.

Index